HOW TO...
Horseback Riding

A step-by-step guide to the
secrets of horseback riding

Written by Caroline Stamps

LONDON, NEW YORK, MUNICH,
MELBOURNE, and DELHI

Senior editor Caroline Stamps
Senior art editor Philip Letsu
US editor Margaret Parrish

Photographer Bob Langrish
Publishing Director Jonathan Metcalf
Associate Publishing Director Liz Wheeler
Art director Phil Ormerod
Publisher Andrew Macintyre
Production editor Ben Marcus
Senior production controller Angela Graef
Jacket editor Manisha Majithia
Jacket designer Laura Brim
Jacket Design Development Manager
Sophia M. T. Turner

Consultant Margaret Linington-Payne

DK INDIA
Project editor Shatarupa Chaudhuri
Project art editor Deep Shikha Walia
Senior art editor Govind Mittal
DTP designer Shanker Prasad, Arvind Kumar
Picture researcher Sakshi Saluja
Managing editor Saloni Talwar
Managing art editor Romi Chakraborty
CTS manager Balwant Singh
Production manager Pankaj Sharma

First published in the United States in 2012
by DK Publishing
375 Hudson Street, New York, New York 10014

Copyright © 2012 Dorling Kindersley Limited

12 13 14 15 16   10 9 8 7 6 5 4 3 2 1
001-184018-05/12

A catalog record for this book
is available from the Library of Congress.

ISBN: 978-0-7566-9243-8
Printed and bound in China by Hung Hing

**Discover more at
www.dk.com**

Contents

" When riding a horse, **YOU ARE IN CHARGE** and the horse will look to you for **reassurance**! "

Introduction

Riding is an activity that many children (and adults!) take up each year. It's a lot of fun, and challenging, too. You'll progress from walking without the help of a leader holding your pony to faster gaits (that's horse speak for "movements") such as a trot and canter, and then to your first jump. As you spend time with horses, you'll discover that no two horses are the same. Always take the time to get to know the horse you are riding.

I'd like to do that!

As you progress with your riding, you will probably want to try different things. There are lots of different styles of riding and you'll need to practice to be good at the one you choose. You can even take part in competitions and win prizes!

Cross-country

Western riding

Trail riding

Dressage

BE PREPARED

Horses are timid animals and will run from danger. Anything they see that is unknown, from a plastic bag on the path ahead to a puddle, may be dangerous. Knowing this will help you to look ahead, figure out the things that may upset them, and reassure them. A prepared rider is a good rider.

Using this book

In between your lessons, this book will let you know what to expect, from grooming your horse or pony to dealing with its tack, and on to the lessons themselves. Saddle up and enjoy yourself!

Before you start

Horses come in a huge variety of breeds, and each breed has distinct characteristics. If you are going to spend time with horses, it is useful to learn a bit about the different types and about their coat colorings and how they communicate.

There are lots of other things that it is useful to know as well. Did you know that there are names for each part of a horse—their "points"? Learn to tell the withers from the poll and the chestnut from the hock! Welcome to the world of all things horse!

Let's speak horse

Horses have their own language. A mare will whinny softly to her foal, but squeal a warning of danger. More importantly, they have a strong body language that is firmly understood by each member of a herd. Understanding this helps us to work with them.

Forming friendships

Horses form close friendships—it's better not to keep them alone. They even groom each other with their teeth to bond with one another. If a horse is not with other horses, then it may form an attachment to a goat or a stable cat. As you get to know different horses, you will also find how different their personalities are, and their individual likes and dislikes.

The curled lip allows the horse to draw the scent of a particular smell into the mouth.

Just a funny face?

If a horse encounters an unusual smell, it will lift its top lip and "smell" with the sensitive membranes inside the lips in addition to smelling through its nostrils. This curling of the lips is called flehmen.

I HEARD THAT!

Horses have excellent hearing. Each ear is controlled by 13 pairs of muscles, making it amazingly mobile. Both ears can move independently. Ear position tells us a lot about a horse's mood.

Pricked forward The horse is interested and listening.

One kept back The horse has picked up a sound from behind.

Back The horse is wary and a little unhappy.

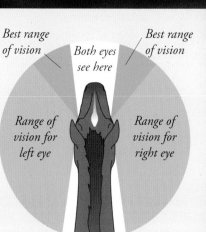

Best range of vision

Best range of vision

Both eyes see here

Range of vision for left eye

Range of vision for right eye

Blind spot behind

I SAW THAT

Horses see well and because their eyes are on the sides of the head, they can see almost 360 degrees. They have a blind spot directly in front of their nose and they cannot see behind them without moving their head to one side… don't creep up on a horse from the back!

Body language

It is important to be confident and relaxed around horses, since they will pick up on mood. They will sense if you are nervous and that makes them nervous.

Horse types and breeds

There are more than 250 breeds of horse, and they range in size from the smallest Falabella to giants such as the Shire and Brabant (or Belgian Draft). Three of the most important breeds are the Arab, the Thoroughbred, and the Barb.

Keep on running
Arabs are a popular choice for long-distance, or endurance, races. This is thanks to their strength and their stamina (their ability to keep going).

The base of an Arab's tail is set high.

An Arab has a short back.

Arab
Famed for its beauty, the Arab's origins have been traced to Arabia and North Africa about 3,000 years ago. Arabs have a small, elegant head, a gracefully curved neck, and their tail is held high when moving. Coats are usually gray, bay, or sorrel.

Thoroughbred
This is the world's fastest breed of horse. The breed dates back to the 17th and 18th centuries in England. In fact, all Thoroughbreds can be traced to three stallions. Most Thoroughbreds are bay, brown, sorrel, or gray.

Fast runners
Thoroughbreds are the best racing horses. Sprinters run short distances while stayers are distance runners.

WHAT WILL I RIDE?
At the riding school, your instructor will choose a quiet horse that is good for a beginner—some breeds are well suited for children. The horse shouldn't be either too large or too small for you.

Welsh pony Friendly and intelligent, they are popular for children. There are four types of Welsh pony.

Haflinger These horses originated in Austria. They are always palominos, with a creamy mane and tail.

Quarter horse These are known for their quiet, calm nature. They are also fast and agile.

A Thoroughbred's shoulder is long and sloping.

Barbs have flat, upright shoulders.

Barb
This is a tough and fast desert horse from North Africa. It can bear high temperatures and can survive with little water. It is usually gray, but is also found in black, brown, sorrel, and bay. The Barb's body is deep at the girth, the tail is set low, and the limbs are slender.

Into battle
Barbs were mainly military horses and were also used in agriculture. They are now used in competitions for riding, racing, and jumping.

Colors and markings

Did you know that a white horse is called a "gray"? Or that a horse with white markings around a hoof has a sock? From bay to black and from piebald to spotted, horses come in a wide range of colors and markings, all of which have a special name. Learning the names will help you to recognize all the horses you meet.

Coronet: white hair that is just above the hoof.

Sock: white hair that reaches halfway up the cannon bone.

Stocking: white hair that reaches up to the knee or the hock.

LEG MARKINGS

Horses may have white hair up to a point on their legs. The length of the white marks determines the name.

Colorful coats
Horses come in lots of different shades, but the most common color is bay. Color is the first thing used to identify a horse. The shades of the coat, skin, mane, tail, and legs are all considered when describing a horse.

Bay These horses have brown coats with a black mane, tail, and legs. The overall color may be dark or light. The mane, tail, and bottom of the legs are called "points."

FACE MARKINGS

Many horses have white markings on their faces. These tend to be similar, but have different names. Three of the most common face markings are shown here. A horse with a completely white face is termed "bald."

Star A regular or irregular spot, in a star shape and set on the head between the eyes, is called a star.

Stripe A narrow strip of white, reaching from above the eyes up to the nostrils, is called a stripe.

Blaze A wide stripe starting above the eyes and running over the muzzle is called a blaze.

Brown Brown horses have mixed black and brown hairs in their coats, with a brown mane, tail, and legs. There may be white markings on the legs or head.

The rings are called dapples.

Dapple gray Light gray hairs form distinct rings on a dark gray coat, or dark gray hairs form rings on a light gray coat. The mane and tail are a lighter shade of gray.

Sorrel These coats show varying shades of reddish-brown, from pale to a rich color. The mane and tail are also reddish-brown.

Gray A gray has black skin with a mix of white and black hairs. The coats come in different shades of gray.

Palomino This is a color, but is often mistaken for a breed. The coat is gold, and the mane and tail are white.

SPOTTED COLOR

Not all horses are one color—some are spotted (also referred to as Appaloosa coloring) or have a patchwork coat. Often, these coats look like they have unique patterns on them.

Skewbald The coat has large patches of color (except black) and white.

Piebald This horse's coat has large patches of black and white.

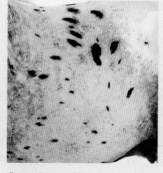

Appaloosa This type of coat usually has dark spots on light hair.

From fetlock to forelock

The different parts of a horse or pony are called its "points." These points make up the animal's shape (its conformation). When people talk about a horse having a "good conformation," this is what they are referring to. It is useful to learn the names of the points, as an instructor may refer to them in a lesson.

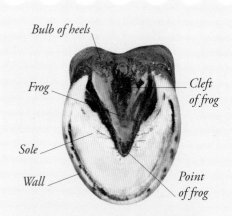

Bulb of heels
Frog
Cleft of frog
Sole
Wall
Point of frog

A FROG IN THE HOOF
A horse's feet are protected by a strong hoof wall. If you look at the underside of the hoof, you will see a V-shaped structure—the frog.

The dock is the bony top part of a horse's tail.

Belly

MEASURING UP
Horses and ponies are measured in hands to the withers, using a measuring stick. A horse stands at more than 14.2 hands, while a pony is anything below this.

The hock bends to allow the hind leg to move forward.

The hoof is sturdy, but stones can become jammed in the sole.

The fetlock joint bends to lift the hoof off the ground.

The lengths of the parts shown by red lines are the same.

All the parts marked by blue lines are of the same length.

Green lines show that fetlock to elbow and elbow to wither are of equal length.

In proportion

When a horse has perfect proportions, it means that some parts of its body are the same length as other parts, as shown in this diagram.

The withers are a sensitive area.

Poll

Forelock

Shoulder

Chestnut

The elbow is a joint like the fetlock and hock.

Knee

Fetlock

Good conformation

A horse's conformation means how it is put together, and good conformation means the horse's points make a perfect shape. Such a horse has a good bone structure, with all its body parts in perfect proportion. This makes it suitable for the work it does.

HEAVY OR LIGHT?

Different types of horse have different characteristics, but the basics of good conformation are always the same. Horses can be divided into three main types: heavy, light, and ponies.

Heavy These horses are large and solidly built, such as this Shire. In the past, they were used as war horses and for work.

Light This category includes most riding horses. There is always some Thoroughbred blood in them.

Pony Ponies are horses that are less than 14.2 hands in height at the withers. A Welsh pony is a popular breed of pony.

Getting ready to ride

Once you have decided you would like to learn to ride, you need to find a local riding school. The following page will give you hints on choosing the right school. You can also take a look at what you (and your horse!) will be wearing. Clothing needs to be comfortable and flexible, while a protective hat and boots are essential.

The riding school

If you want to begin riding, you need to find a riding school. A friend may be able to suggest a local school. Visit the school before booking a lesson, so you know what to expect. A good school will give you the confidence to learn and improve.

Riding school horses are usually older, experienced animals.

THE TACK ROOM
Every riding school should have a well-organized tack room, which should be kept neat. The tack should be clean and hanging on brackets.

At the riding school
When you first visit a riding school, look to see if the stable block and the yard are tidy. Do the horses and ponies look healthy and alert? Are all riders in riding hats? Do the people working there seem friendly?

INDOORS OR OUTDOORS?

Riding schools should have an enclosed area in which you can learn to ride safely. This is called an arena and it is usually in the open. There may be an indoor school, which is useful for riding when it is raining.

Indoor An indoor arena is handy for riding if it is wet and windy outside.

Outdoor You will be riding inside a fenced area, which may be a portion of a larger area.

A school's horses and ponies should be calm.

Getting ready to ride

When you arrive for your lesson, you will be fitted with a hard hat. You will be told who you are riding, and may see your pony being tacked up. Relax and enjoy yourself. It always helps to say hello to your pony.

What to wear

Riders need to wear certain pieces of clothing for safety. For shows, riders dress up. But whether for a show or for everyday riding, you need to be in comfortable clothes that stretch as you move.

Properly dressed
Try on your outfit before you start riding. All that you wear must fit properly. The jodhpurs should have extra padding to protect your legs.

BODY PROTECTION
You will sometimes see riders wearing body protectors, especially if they are going on cross-country treks.

Safety gear
Body protectors fit over clothes and protect the body in case of a fall. Always wear one if you are jumping.

On top A body protector is usually worn on top of your other clothes.

A high collar protects your neck.

IT'S RAINING!
If you ride in the rain, you need a waterproof coat. Don't ride with a jacket or coat unzipped or unbuttoned—it could flap in the wind and scare your horse.

Material It is best if the coat is made of a breathable material.

A safety harness helps to keep the hat in position.

Gloves

Gloves help you to hold the reins properly, especially in wet weather, and they keep your hands from getting dry and sore. Riding gloves are usually made from cotton, nylon, or wool, with a surface that helps you keep a tight grip.

Riding crop

Hard hat

A securely fitting riding hat is essential, so that if you do fall you are protected. Always use a hat with a safety harness. Many countries have a safety mark for riding hats that guarantees a hat's strength.

T-shirts should not be too tight or you will not be able to move freely.

Jodhpurs

These riding trousers are the most comfortable things you can wear for riding. They are padded to stop your leg from rubbing on the saddle. They are stretchy, too, so that you can bend more easily to mount and dismount.

Riding boots

Riding boots have a slight heel, which prevents your foot from slipping through the stirrup, and a smooth sole. They may be long or short, but will always cover the ankle, and they don't have buckles or laces (which would catch in the stirrups).

Grooming your pony

Grooming relaxes a horse and keeps its coat and hooves clean. It also allows you to check the horse for signs of injury or infection. Stabled horses are groomed daily, while horses that live outside require less grooming (or you will remove too much of the grease from their coat that makes it waterproof).

THE GROOMING KIT

Each horse should have its own grooming kit, with the items in the kit kept in a container together. A good kit includes these items:

Dandy brush Used on the body to remove mud and loose hair.

Body brush Softer bristles make this ideal for the head, mane, and tail.

Rubber curry comb Used to remove dried mud.

Sponges Use one sponge for the head and another for the dock.

Metal curry comb This is used for cleaning brushes.

Hoof pick Used to clear the hooves of mud and stones.

Sweat scraper Helps remove sweat after exercise.

Each hoof needs to be cleaned out with a hoof pick

Always brush following the way the hair grows.

LOOK AFTER YOUR BRUSHES

Clean your brushes by scraping them against a metal curry comb. Try to do this away from the horse, so the dust and hairs that come out do not blow back on the horse. Never use a metal comb on a horse or pony.

Clean the nose and eyes with a damp sponge.

Daily grooming

A field-kept pony usually just requires a quick cleaning with a dandy brush to remove dried mud. If this is not removed, the dirt could rub under the girth or bridle and cause sores. You should also brush away any tangles from the mane and tail.

A look at tack

The headpiece holds the bridle in place.

Just like people, horses vary in size and shape, so each horse needs its own set of tack, which has been carefully fitted. Poorly fitting tack can cause sores and discomfort, which will lead to a horse behaving badly.

The browband stops the bridle from slipping backwards.

The cheekpiece is attached to the headpiece and bit.

Storing Do not store the bridle in a damp place because the leather will become moldy.

Reins are attached to the rings on the bit.

The bit passes through the horse's mouth.

A martingale can be used to prevent a horse throwing its head up.

Bridle
The bridle fits the head to hold the bit in place, which gives the rider control. Bridles are mainly of two types—the snaffle bridle and the double bridle. This horse is wearing a snaffle bridle.

Halters and lead ropes
These are used to lead a pony to and from the field, or around the stable. This gives control when not riding.

Saddle

This needs to be specially fitted, so that it is comfortable for the horse. Padded panels keep pressure off the horse's spine. There are different saddles for special horse events, such as jumping and dressage.

The numnah absorbs sweat and grease.

The pommel is the front part of the saddle.

Horn

Cantle

The stitching that holds the buckle to the girth must be checked regularly.

Fender

A Western saddle's girth is called a cinch.

English saddle The English saddle is used around the world for the English riding discipline.

Western saddle The saddle for Western riding is usually more decorative than the English saddle.

Rugs

Some rugs are worn in the stable; some are worn outside. Some are fly sheets for summer wear, while others are waterproof. Here, the horse is wearing a fly sheet to discourage flies.

Girth

A girth can be made of leather, cotton, string, or a synthetic material. The girth passes under a horse's belly and has buckles at each end to hold the saddle in position.

Stirrup irons

These are attached to the saddle with stirrup leathers. Stirrups must be of the correct width so that your feet do not get stuck in them.

CLEAN TACK

Tack needs regular cleaning, otherwise it picks up dirt and becomes uncomfortable to wear.

Polishing the metal Wash the stirrup irons and bit, and wipe them with a damp sponge. Then rub metal polish on them and rub them with a soft cloth to make them gleam.

Cleaning the saddle Take off the girth, stirrup leathers, and irons. Wash with a damp cloth or sponge to remove grease and dirt. Then rub saddle soap into the leather.

Cleaning the bridle Dip a sponge in water and squeeze out the excess water. Take the bridle apart and wipe each strap with a damp sponge. Apply saddle soap.

25

PUT ON A BRIDLE

Stand at the pony's nearside. Undo the noseband and throatlatch.

1. Fasten the halter around the pony's neck and put the reins over its head. Grasp the bridle below the headpiece and slide your left thumb into the corner of the pony's mouth, then guide the bit in.

2. Put the headpiece over the pony's ears, and place the ears through the gap between the headpiece and browband. Gently take the forelock from under the browband.

3. Fasten the noseband and the throatlatch. You should be able to slip a hand's width between the throatlatch and the pony, and two fingers between the noseband and face.

Tacking up

Before a horse is ready to ride, it needs to be tacked up. This means putting on its saddle and bridle, after it has been groomed. A well-trained horse should stand quietly while being tacked up.

Panel

Sweat flap

Look after the saddle

If you need to put a saddle on the ground, always place it carefully on the pommel and lean the cantle against a wall. Use the girth to protect the cantle.

Near fore is the front left leg.

Off fore is the front right leg.

Near hind is the back left leg.

Off hind is the back right leg.

Useful terms

Nearside refers to the left-hand side of the horse's body, while offside is its right-hand side.

PUT ON A SADDLE *HOW TO...*

Check that the stirrup irons are run up, and the girth is folded over the saddle and attached to its right-hand side.

1. Start from the pony's nearside shoulder. Gently slide the saddle and numnah onto the pony's back, holding them at the front and back.

2. Pull the numnah up into the saddle's gullet. Drop the girth down the pony's side, and pass it through the numnah's loop. Reach for the girth and fasten it in position.

All done!

Once you have tacked up, check all the buckles. The bit should sit high enough to fit snugly into the corners of the mouth, but without putting too much strain on the mouth. Make sure the noseband, browband, and bit are straight. Tighten the girth, then gently pull each foreleg forward. This releases any skin that may be caught.

In the saddle

Horseback riding is a lot of fun. You learn to control an animal that is far larger and more powerful than yourself. It takes patience, since you have to learn to "listen" to the horse and respond to its actions, but it's incredibly rewarding.

This section of the book will give you lots of hints and tips about getting started with your riding lessons. Remember, at the back of the book you will find a glossary that will help you to learn the words used in horseback riding.

MOUNT

Mount by putting one foot in the stirrup and springing up.

1. Facing the tail, stand with your left shoulder next to the pony's left shoulder. Hold the reins in your left hand, just in front of the saddle. Use your right hand to turn the back edge of the stirrup iron toward you.

2. Put your left foot into the stirrup and turn your body to face the pony's side. Reach up, take a hold of the saddle, and push off the ground with your right foot so that you are standing in the stirrup.

3. Swing your right leg over the pony's back. Turn your body to face forward and gently lower yourself into the saddle. Feel for the other stirrup with your right foot. Never let go of the reins.

Let's begin

Getting on and off a pony safely is called mounting and dismounting. Your instructor will check that the girth is tight enough, and that the pony is standing still. You will either mount from the ground, perhaps with a leg up, or from a mounting block.

Sit and relax

The instructor will make sure that the pony stands still while you get on. Try and relax once you have mounted and are sitting on the pony. It may seem strange at first, but you will soon feel comfortable.

A leg up: another way to mount

Gather the reins in your left hand, and put your right hand on the saddle. Bend your left knee so that the instructor can hold your leg and help you up as you swing your right leg over the saddle.

When you are seated, hold the reins with both hands.

Tighten the girth so that the saddle does not slide around.

You may need to adjust the length of the stirrup leathers.

DISMOUNT

There are different ways to dismount. You may take both feet out of the stirrups, or keep one foot in the stirrup. Always dismount in the way your instructor teaches you. Try not to prod your pony in the side with your toes while getting off!

1. Take both feet out of the stirrups and hold the reins in your left hand.

2. Lean forward and swing your right leg over the pony's back.

3. Bend your knees slightly, slide down, and land with both feet together, trying to face forward.

First steps

Once you are in the saddle, try to relax. A relaxed posture helps the horse to move under you, and helps it to respond to your commands. Your instructor will help you achieve the correct position so that you and your horse are well balanced.

On the lunge
You may have early lessons on the lunge rein. This long rein allows the instructor to control your horse, so you can work on improving your position in the saddle.

Holding the reins
Hold the reins slightly apart, with your thumbs on top. They should pass between your fingers as shown. Make sure the reins are not twisted. Never pull— remember, they are attached to the bit in your pony's mouth.

A good seat
Hold the reins in both hands, and sit upright, in the middle of the saddle. Keep your head up, your elbows in, and your heels down. Look ahead, between the pony's ears.

Look straight ahead.

Make a straight line from your elbows to the reins.

Keep your back straight.

Walk on

Sit up straight, and push with your seat. Close your legs on the pony's sides. As you feel the pony respond, let your hands move forward a little. Once the pony is walking, allow your hands to move backward and forward with the pony's head. Let your lower half move with the pony.

Keep your arms relaxed.

The stirrup should be under the widest part—the ball—of your foot.

FUN WITH EXERCISES

Your teacher may ask you to do some warm-up exercises so that you get to know your horse better. These are always fun to do.

In control

Aids are signals that a horse is trained to understand—it is the way in which you "talk" to your horse. Your legs, hands, voice, and body position act as natural aids. Closing the fingers on the reins tells your horse to stop. A gentle squeeze of the legs tells the pony to walk on.

On the leading rein
For your first few lessons, someone will lead your horse. If you are nervous, there will be a neck strap—hold this in addition to holding the reins until you are used to the movement.

Stop and start
It's good to know you can stop and start your pony. Practice stopping between two parallel poles spaced a few steps apart.

USEFUL TERMS
The arena is the area in which you will ride. It is a safe, enclosed space. Once in the arena in a lesson, there are a number of frequently used terms that you will soon become familiar with.

Change the rein This is when the lead horse changes the direction in a school, and the others follow.

Inside/outside The inside leg is the one on the inside of a bend. This can refer to your leg or hand, or the horse's legs.

Right rein/left rein You are riding on the left rein if your left hand is on the inside of the arena.

How to turn

You need to steer your pony. It's very helpful to learn to look where you want to go—this helps to shift your body slightly, which a well-trained horse will respond to.

The rider is exaggerating the hand movement to show you need to think of opening the rein when turning rather than pulling back.

Squeeze the pony's sides with your legs to show that you want to go forward.

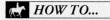
TAKE A RIGHT TURN

Here are the aids you have to use if you want to turn right.

Using your hands Feel the right rein gently, until the pony turns its head right. As it turns, let your left hand move forward. Keep contact with the pony's mouth.

Using your outside leg Place your left leg (your outside leg for a right turn) behind the girth. This stops the pony from swinging out its hindquarters as it turns.

Using your inside leg Press inward with your right leg (your inside leg for a right turn). This encourages the pony to go forward. Imagine that you are turning the pony around this leg.

Riding in the school

Horse riding arenas (also called "schools") have letters on boards around the edge, which act as useful guides for starting and finishing exercises that your teacher will ask you to do. The letters are called markers. They are always the same.

Keep a distance
You'll probably start riding in a small group. The first rider is called the leading file. It's important to keep a horse's length between your pony and the one in front.

THE ARENA
While practicing, you'll get familiar with the markers that surround the arena. This is a standard arena that is ideal for school exercises.

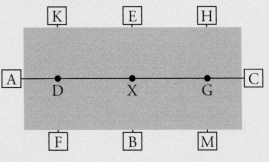

Arena The letters around the arena are A, K, E, H, C, M, B, and F. Along the center are D, X, and G.

PASSING A PONY

When riding in an arena with others, you will sometimes need to pass another rider. To pass a pony that is coming toward you, leave at least a pony's width between you and pass left to the left.

Left-hand rule A good way to pass one another is to make sure that your left hand is on the side of the other rider's left hand.

EXERCISES

In your lessons, you'll be asked to do different exercises using the markers as guides. These include riding in circles and half-circles, and in figure eights.

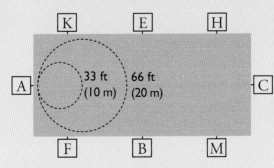

Circles You'll ride in circles of either 66 ft (20 m) or 33 ft (10 m) in diameter in a walk, trot, or canter.

Figure eights These are a good way to practice changing the rein, which means changing direction.

Learning to trot

Once you are confident with a walk, you will want to learn a faster pace. The next step is learning to trot. You may find it feels a little bumpy at first, but once you pick up the horse's rhythm and rise up and down in the saddle (at a rising trot), you will find it is a comfortable movement. You will also learn the sitting trot.

Practice the rising trot
While your pony is standing still, try rising and sitting again in the saddle. Push down on the stirrups with your heels as you go up.

TROT ON!
A trotting pony moves its legs in diagonal pairs. This pony's red bandages clearly show the movement of these pairs.

1 Notice how one front hoof and the back hoof on the opposite side are on the ground at the same time.

2 On the next stride, the pairs on the ground at the same time have changed. The pony is in a steady trot.

1 When asking your pony to move forward into trot, shorten your reins slightly. This will stop them from being slack when the pony moves into trot, which helps your control.

2 Remain seated until you have settled into a rhythm with your pony's movement. Keep an even contact with the pony's mouth, and try to keep your legs still.

SITTING TROT

It's good to be able to ride at a sitting as well as a rising trot. One of the ways in which you can improve your sitting trot is by riding without stirrups. Your instructor may put your pony on a long lunge rein to do this.

No stirrups! Riding a sitting trot without stirrups improves balance and confidence.

Rise up gently— you're aiming to achieve a slight movement with your hips.

A steady rhythm

It can be difficult to find the horse's rhythm for a rising trot. Trotting is a two-tone gait or movement, so try to pick up the 1-2, 1-2 rhythm. It may help to count "One-two, one-two."

Try not to pull on the reins to find your balance. As a beginner, this is hard to avoid, but it is important, since it helps your horse to move smoothly.

Try to keep your weight in your heels, even when you have to use your legs.

❝ Remember to **LOOK FORWARD**, between your pony's ears. Keep your **back straight**, and enjoy! **❞**

3 Once you feel the pony's rhythm, begin to rise and sit. This should feel like an easy movement—you should be matching the movement of your pony's front legs.

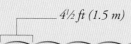

Learning to canter

Once you have learned to trot, you will probably want to learn to canter. Canter is a comfortable pace, with a slight rocking motion, and a three-beat rhythm. Horses find it quite easy to maintain this pace—it is faster than a trot but slower than a gallop.

DIFFERENT PACES

In trot as well as canter, a horse's movement creates a motion like a wave. The difference between the two is the length of that wave, which is the horse's stride.

4½ ft (1.5 m)

Working trot The working trot is the horse's natural pace. The horse covers about 4½ ft (1.5 m) in a step.

12 ft (3.5 m)

Working canter In the working canter, the horse picks up its natural rhythm and covers about 12 ft (3.5 m) in a stride.

Ready to canter

It helps if you plan ahead for the change from trot to canter. Sit up, and always remember not to pull on the reins as you move from trot into the canter. Make sure your horse's back can move freely.

1 If your seat is balanced, go into an active but unhurried sitting trot.

2 Sit up, squeeze with both legs, and go into a canter.

> "Bring the horse **BACK TO TROT** if you or the horse feel **unbalanced**."

GALLOPING

Gallop is a horse's fastest gait. It is very similar to cantering, with one main difference. There are four footfalls in a stride in a gallop, instead of the three footfalls in a canter.

Ask for gallop Build a powerful, forward canter until your horse speeds up.

Leading leg

To strike off into a canter, the trot must be active and balanced. Once in a canter, the horse stretches one foreleg in front of the other legs. This is called the leading leg. A horse can lead with either leg—this horse is leading with its right leg. If moving around a school, the leading leg should be on the inside of the school to help the horse's balance.

3 Allow the power of the canter to move your hips.

4 To maintain the canter, keep your legs in place, and squeeze, if necessary.

5 To go back to a trot, keep your legs on, sit up, and close your fingers around the reins.

My first jump

Once you have learned to trot and canter, and you are confident about turning your pony, you can learn to jump. Jumping is lots of fun. It may look fast, but it is simply a matter of balance and confidence. You can improve both by using trotting poles.

Trotting poles

You may have used trotting poles while learning to trot to establish a good rhythm. Trotting poles give you a chance to practice a jumping position. They also help you to get used to your pony's stride changing as it moves over an obstacle.

Keep your back straight and your head up.

Never pull on the pony's mouth to find your balance.

Let your weight sink down into your heels.

A good jumping position

Practice your jumping position in the saddle before you begin jumping. The position is known as two point, or half seat, because you are shifting your weight onto two points— your legs. Exercises based on this will help to strengthen the muscles you use for jumping.

Tips for jumping

When learning, always ride at the jump straight on. As your pony jumps, let your weight sink down into your heels and begin to lean forward. Then begin to sit up as the horse lands.

Your first jump

You will learn to jump over a pair of crossed poles. A crossed pole jump encourages the horse to line up with the center of the jump, where it is lowest. The height of the poles can be raised as you progress.

Remember to keep your head up.

Allow the horse freedom of movement in its head and neck.

PROGRESS IN JUMPING

Most horses and ponies are happy to jump a range of obstacles, but you must advance from simple jumps to difficult ones.

❶

Starting out Trotting poles are evenly spaced. They are usually about nine footsteps apart.

❷

First jump Crossed poles are an easier jump when you are learning.

❸

A challenge Once you gain experience, all kinds of jumps are possible, such as two fences together, called a double.

Shorten your stirrups

Before you jump, your instructor will suggest you shorten your stirrups by a couple of holes. It helps you to keep your balance as the horse jumps.

Keep your foot in the stirrups while adjusting or tightening them.

Let's go hacking!

Once you feel confident in the saddle, it's lots of fun to go for a ride away from the riding school. This is called hacking. Horses enjoy this—they are usually a little livelier than they might be in a school.

The instructor will warn you about low branches, or tree roots that may trip the pony.

To signal to a car that you are going right, pass the reins into your left hand and hold out your right arm. Do the opposite if turning left.

To be clearly visible when riding on roads, use a fluorescent belt or jacket. Your horse may have fluorescent leg bands.

On the road

Always be aware of what's going on around you when you are riding, and even more so if riding on a road. Check behind you before moving off, or moving out around parked cars or other obstacles. Look ahead for things that may make your horse nervous—there may be construction work, for instance— and keep to the side of the road.

Trail riding

When riding in the country, you are likely to follow special trails known as bridle paths. Riding on uneven ground helps improve balance. But look out for sharp stones that could hurt your pony's hooves.

GATE SKILLS

One of the obstacles you may meet while hacking is a gate. It takes a lot of practice to open and close a gate from the back of a horse. Watch how your instructor does it.

Keep a safe distance from each other so you have time to react if the pony in front makes a sudden stop.

 **HOW TO...**

GO UP AND DOWN

Hacking helps develop your riding skills as you meet situations you don't come across in a school. Move your body to make it easier for the horse when you go up or down a steep bank.

1. Bend your upper body forward if you are going up.

2. When going back down, sit upright and slightly back.

FANCY MOVES

Horses that are trained to respond to commands through Western riding can perform all kinds of amazing movements. This is known as reining.

Roll-back In this move, the horse turns 180 degrees without stopping, heading off in the opposite direction.

Spin In this difficult move, the horse puts its hind leg firmly on the ground and spins around 360 degrees.

Sliding stop In a dramatic show of skill, horse and rider slide to a sudden halt from a gallop.

Western riding

"Long leg, remember your neck reining, shift your seat…." You'll hear these commands from your instructor if you take up Western riding. Western riders sit deep in the saddle, with their legs almost straight. This way of riding developed in countries where horses were used to herd cattle.

Western stirrups are sometimes covered with leather.

A Western saddle is heavier than an English saddle. It spreads the weight over a larger area of the horse's back.

What is neck reining?

Western riders turn the horse by using the reins on the horse's neck, in addition to shifting their weight in the saddle. The horse is trained to respond to the gentle pressure this makes. To turn left, you would use the right rein against the horse's neck and shift your weight to the left. The reins are held in one hand. When herding, this means that one hand is free to rope in the cattle.

First lessons

You and your horse will need to take special classes for Western training. Western riders traditionally wear wide-brimmed hats, but it is safer to wear a safety helmet.

There are two main types of Western bridle. This type has a browband. Others have an earpiece that loops around one ear.

COMPETITION!

The skills of a Western-style rider and horse are shown at various shows around the world. The horse is judged for its agility and speed. There are also contests for cowboys called rodeos.

Protection

Horses wear special leg equipment at Western competitions, where moves such as a sliding stop are shown.

Sliding plate This flat shoe helps with the sudden moves.

Skid boots These boots protect the horse's fetlocks.

More fun with horses

Once you are more confident in the saddle, there is a lot of fun to be had with competitions and events. It's exciting to try to win a rosette! Try entering a gymkhana, or practice some dressage skills. If you love being with horses, you may consider working with horses in the future. In this section of the book, take a look at some of the possible careers.

Preparing for a show

A braided mane looks neat and tidy.

Your first show is likely to be a small, local competition. You and your horse need to look good for it. Make sure that your horse is fit and clean, and your clothes and tack are in good condition. There will be different classes, which separate the horses depending on things such as size and age.

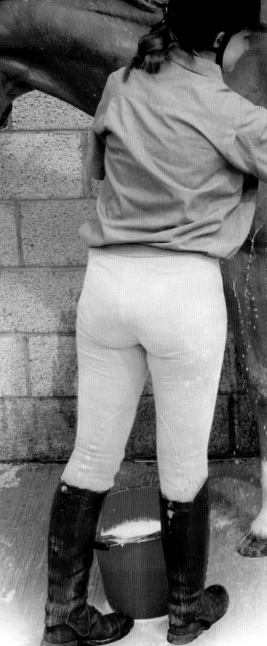

🐎 **HOW TO...**

BRAID A MANE
Start by dampening the mane with a brush dipped in water. This makes the mane easier to handle. Always work from the top of the neck toward the shoulders.

1. Equal bunches Divide the mane into equal-sized bunches. Put a rubber band around each until you are ready to braid that section.

2. Braid the sections Divide each bunch into three and braid tightly. Put a rubber band at the bottom of the braids.

3. Roll and hold Fold each braid under and under again, then use a needle and thread to sew each braid in place.

Washing your pony

It's good to wash your pony for a show. Choose a warm day. Mix a little horse shampoo in a bucket of lukewarm water. Wet the coat, then soap the mane and neck. Gently sponge the body, face, legs, and tail. Rinse with clean water, remove excess water with a sweat scraper, and towel dry. Don't let your pony get cold.

Patterns can be made on a horse's hind quarters.

After washing, brush the hooves with hoof oil.

Tails can be braided.

BRAID A TAIL

You can only braid a full tail. It's not easy, so watch how it is done a few times. Dampen the top half of the tail and take in just a few hairs at a time.

1. Begin to braid Working from the top, take small sections of hair from the center and each side of the tail. Braid these and bring in small sections as you work down.

2. Keep going Continue braiding, adding small sections from each side and from the center as you go. You would normally braid to the end of your pony's dock.

3. A neat finish Continue with just the central section. When finished, loop this long braid under and secure with a needle and thread.

Games on horseback

Imagine party games but on horseback, and that will give you a sense of what happens with mounted games. You can play these games at events called gymkhanas. The games are fast-paced and fun, and a wide variety are played the world over.

Pole bending race
In this race, two sets of poles are set into the ground in a straight line. Mounted riders weave in and out of the lines, trying not to touch the poles.

Ball and bucket race
For this game, two teams of riders race to collect one object (such as a ball or a small bean bag) at a time, before riding on to drop it in a bucket. There are usually several balls and the first team to finish wins.

Burst the balloon

This noisy game is also called "bang a balloon." Balloons are attached to the ground. Two teams of riders take turns using a long stick to burst the balloons—the more balloons a team bursts, the more points it wins.

Flag race

This is a simple game. Each rider collects a flag and has to drop it into a bucket or a container before racing back to the finish line. If the rider misses the container, he must retrieve the flag and start again.

Stepping-stones

Test your balancing skills in this exciting game! Riders have to dismount their horses and run lightly over a series of upturned buckets. Then, they vault back into the saddle and finish the race.

POLO

This game is like field hockey played on horseback. Two teams try to score goals against each other using long sticks called mallets. The aim is to hit a small white ball into a goal.

Cross-country

Cross-country riding is exciting and fast-paced, taking the horse and rider across all sorts of obstacles. Riders start with classes on easier courses and after years of training, they are ready for big competitions. It's fun to take part, once you are confident in the saddle.

A test of strength

A cross-country course is often followed for fun, or it may form a part of a competition to prove the speed, jumping ability, and endurance capability of a horse. A good cross-country rider must be able to ride fast, but keep a steady rhythm and stay in control.

Stirrups should be slightly shorter than for normal jumping.

JUMPS TO EXPECT

A rider has to cross lots of different jumps on a real course. Here are some of the more advanced jumps.

Wall This is a straightforward jump, but the wall is solid and it must be crossed with care.

Pheasant feeder This should be approached at a good speed so the horse builds up for a powerful jump.

Hedge The horse needs to clear the top of the hedge. This is difficult when it cannot see what is on the other side.

Zigzag A rider may jump over the straight section or directly through the "V" if the fence has flags at either end.

YOU'RE OUT!

If a rider falls off the horse, they are eliminated. However, a horse can refuse a jump up to three times before the horse and rider are eliminated. If you fall, try to do a somersault so that you land in a squatting position.

A red flag indicates the right-hand side of the jump.

Watch the flags

You will be eliminated for jumping a fence in the wrong direction—flags mark the way. The red flag needs to be on your right and the white flag on your left. The rider should walk the course before a competition begins to know the flag positions.

Riding across-country

The horse and the rider must focus on the jump well ahead of the fence. As the horse takes off, just go with its movement and give it more freedom of rein, if necessary. Let your body come upright without hitting the horse's back and keep your legs in contact with the horse when you land.

Dressage

Dressage consists of carefully controlled movements that show a horse's obedience, athletic ability, and balance. It is the result of teamwork between the horse and rider. If you enjoy it, there are plenty of dressage competitions.

DRESSAGE ARENA
Top dressage riders work in a larger area than beginners. The area is clearly marked, with letter markers placed outside the arena. The arena is enclosed by white boards.

If you have long hair, then tie it in a hairnet.

“ Check the **RULES regarding tack** in a competition, since they are usually **specific. ”**

The horse's hooves are oiled for competitions.

Looking sharp
A dressage rider and horse have to be clean and tidy. A beginner wears a jacket with a shirt and tie. Jodhpurs have to be beige or white.

Who can do dressage?

Anyone who can ride! A horse needs to be able to obey basic commands and keep to a steady rhythm when trotting and cantering around a 22-yard (20-m) circle. Beyond that, dressage is a matter of practice.

The horse has to move confidently and with purpose.

The rider salutes the judge when at halt.

Halt!

All dressage tests end with a halt, so a good stop and stand is important. If a horse is fidgety, or won't obey its rider's commands, the rider needs to work with the horse to improve this.

PRACTICE MAKES PERFECT

A dressage rider needs to be able to feel what the horse is doing. Top dressage horses are trained in their skills for years, but it's simple to pick up basic dressage movements, such as leg yields and serpentines.

A controlled canter Judges look for balanced, even steps.

Working with horses

If you enjoy riding and working with horses, you may think about making it a job when you grow up. There are quite a lot of horse-related careers. Take a look at some of these.

Flat racing jockey
Jockeys are professionals who ride horses in races. Flat racing is done on a level track over a fixed distance. You are likely to start out as an apprentice jockey under a trainer before you race independently.

Riding instructor
To be an instructor, you must train for several years, improve your riding skills and horse knowledge, and take teaching exams. You also need patience and the ability to encourage a nervous beginner.

Professional show jumper
A show-jumping course tests riding skills as well as a horse's jumping ability. Penalties are awarded for knocking down a fence, refusals, running around a fence, or falling. A successful show jumper will have spent many years in training with a particular horse.

Horse whisperer

As a horse whisperer, you will "talk" to horses in a certain way. Horse whisperers learn a horse's body language and train horses using gentle methods. Your job will be to make the horse feel calm and safe so that it learns easily.

FARRIER

Like your nails, a horse's hooves grow and need to be trimmed. Some horses are fitted with shoes. Care of a horse's hooves is the work of a farrier, who usually travels to work at different stables.

A FARRIER'S TOOLS

A farrier uses various instruments to trim a horse's hooves and fit its shoes.

Drawing knife Used to trim the hoof wall.

Hammer Metal head drives the nails in when shoeing a horse.

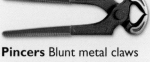

Pincers Blunt metal claws help to grip and remove old shoes.

Rasp This metal file is used to level the hoof before shoeing.

On show

Some riding schools have become famous the world over for their skills. The Spanish School in Vienna and the Cadre Noir in France are two of the best known. Riders at both schools spend many years training their horses to perform spectacular movements, including some amazing leaps into the air.

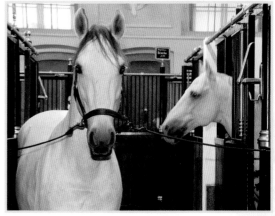

A peek at the horses

The Spanish School is famous for its Lipizzaner stallions. These horses are considered noble, and are perfectly suited for classical horsemanship. They come to the school when they are four years old and are trained for six years.

A peek at the riders

The Spanish School accepts one pupil each year from a large pool of applicants. Applicants have to be at least 16 years of age, and have basic riding skills. The pupils spend a few years learning about care of the horses and equipment, as well as receiving riding lessons. It is hard work.

It's a great show!

The Spanish Riding School has many shows that people can go and watch. The School Quadrille, which is a performance that uses eight horses, is famous. Some of the great moves that the riders perform are the *levade* and the *courbette*. All riders wear a traditional, brown tailcoat uniform with a special hat.

This horse is performing a spectacular leap called "capriole".

OLYMPICS
Riders who excel at the schools have often taken part in Olympic riding events. Didier Courrège is famous for winning a gold medal in the 2004 Olympics. He is part of the Cadre Noir equestrian (horseback riding) display team.

Airs above the ground
The riders of the two schools perform spectacular dressage moves. These are called "airs above the ground," since the horses jump into the air while performing them. One such jump is the *croupade*, as seen here.

Glossary

aids The means by which a rider communicates with a horse, using, for example, weight, legs, voice, and hands.

arena An enclosed area in which people receive riding lessons. It is also known as a "school."

bit The part of the *bridle* that fits into a horse's mouth. It is usually made of metal.

bridle A horse's head harness.

browband This is part of the *bridle*. It lies across the horse's forehead and prevents the *bridle* from slipping back.

canter A three-beat *gait*.

change the rein A command from a riding instructor that tells you to change the direction your horse is moving around the *arena*.

conformation A horse or a pony's shape.

cross-country course A course that takes a horse and rider over a variety of natural jumps, such as walls, fences, and gates.

dock A horse's tailbone.

dressage A method of improving a horse's obedience by schooling him. It consists of carefully controlled movements that demonstrate the balance and agility of a horse and rider.

farrier A person who cares for a horse's hooves.

flat racing Racing that takes place on a level course, with no jumps or obstacles.

flehmen A facial expression produced when a horse pulls up its top lip to "sniff" the air. This is done in response to an unusual smell or taste.

gallop A four-beat *gait*, this is the fastest movement of all.

gait A type of movement, such as *trot*.

girth The strap that holds the saddle and runs around the horse's stomach.

groom To brush a horse's coat and pick out of its feet.

gymkhana Games that take place on horseback between teams of riders.

hack A ride outside the riding school, in the countryside.

halter A piece of *tack* that fits around a horse's head and is used for leading a horse to or from the field. It is also used to tie the horse to a ring in the stable.

hands The form of measurement used to describe a horse or pony's height. One hand is 4 in (10 cm).

horse whisperer A person trained to respond to a horse using the methods horses use to communicate among themselves.

inside leg This refers to the horse or rider's leg that is on the inside of an arena, as the horse works around the arena.

jodhpurs These are full-length, padded riding pants.

leading file The first horse and rider in a riding school lesson.

leading leg The front leg that reaches farther forward when a horse is *cantering*. On a bend, the horse should be leading with its *inside leg*.

left rein Moving off in an arena with the open area on your left and the fence on your right. You will move in a counterclockwise direction.

lunge rein A long rein that means a horse can be controlled by a trainer who is standing on the ground. The horse works in a circle around the trainer.

near fore A horse's front left leg.

near hind A horse's rear left leg.

neckstrap An extra strap that is added to provide support to a beginner rider.

noseband The part of the *bridle* that goes around the horse's nose.

numnah Soft pad that is sometimes used under a saddle.

off fore A horse's front right leg.

off hind A horse's rear right leg.

outside leg This refers to the horse or rider's leg that is on the fenced side of the arena, as the horse works around the arena.

points The different parts of a horse or pony, such as its fetlock.

polo A game that is played on horseback with long-handled mallets and a small white ball.

posture The way a rider sits when in the saddle.

reins Long straps that run from the *bit* and are held by the rider.

reining A type of *Western riding* that includes competition moves such as a sliding stop.

right rein Moving off in an arena with the open area on your right and the fence on your left. You will move in a clockwise direction.

rodeo A competition popular in North America in which cowboys demonstrate skills that are related to riding and to handling cattle.

rosette A badge given to winning horses and riders at equestrian events.

showjumping A competition that takes place in an enclosed arena in which horses and riders compete over a series of jumps.

stirrups Metal supports that hang from the saddle and into which the riders place their feet.

tack Equipment used for riding, such as the saddle and *bridle*.

trot A two-beat *gait* in which the horse's legs move in diagonal pairs.

Western riding A style of riding in which the rider's leg position is kept long, and the horse responds to pressure of the *reins* on its neck. The *reins* are held in one hand.

withers The top of a horse's shoulders. Horses and ponies are measured to their withers.

Index

Acknowledgments

Dorling Kindersley would like to thank the following for their help in the production of this book: Toby and Jennifer Greenbury, owners of Checkendon Equestrian Centre, Lovegrove's Lane, Checkendon, Reading, RG8 0NE (www.checkendonequestrian.co.uk) for their kind permission to photograph the book there; special thanks to manager Linda Tarrant for her time and invaluable guidance during the photoshoot; our models: Ellie, India, Jessie, Joshua, and Lily; photographer Bob Langrish; Margaret Linington-Payne, Director of Standards at the British Horse Society, for her patience and expertise; Mahipal Singh and Aanchal Singal for design assistance; and a thank you also to the horses and ponies we used, especially Tod, Isabella, Homer, Mouse, and Banjo. Thank you also to Claire and Sophie, Tanya, Belinda, and Gemma.

Margaret Linington-Payne is Director of Standards for the British Horse Society. She is a BHSI and a qualified teacher with a Masters Degree in Education. A BHS Chief Assessor she has, in the past, worked in the Middle East and at Hartpury College in Gloucestershire, England. She has also been the proprietor and chief instructor of a BHS Approved Riding School and Examination Centre.

Picture credits

The publisher would like to thank the following for their kind permission to reproduce their photographs: (Key: a-above; b-below/bottom; c-center; f-far; l-left; r-right; t-top)Alamy Images: catnap / Alamy 52cr, Juniors Bildarchiv / Alamy 8tr, National Geographic Image Collection / Alamy 60cl, Mark J. Barrett / Alamy 58tl, Network Photographers / Alamy 53br, Insadco Photography / Alamy 60tr; Allstar: Paul Mcfegan 61tr; Animal Photography: vloo 61br; Ardea: Johan de Meester 11tc; Corbis: Ocean / Corbis 34bl, Salah Ibrahim / epa / Corbis 10tr, Frederic Haslin / TempSport / Corbis 58bl, Kit Houghton / Corbis 56tr, 59cr, Wolfgang Kaehler / Corbis 8c, William Manning / Corbis 11tl, Leo Mason / Corbis 53tr, Roland Schlager / epa / Corbis 60–61, Chase Swift / Corbis 11tr; Dorling Kindersley: Dan Bannister 7tr; Getty Images: Alan Crowhurst / Stringer / Getty Images 58–59, Alvis Upitis 47cl, Bongarts / Christof Koepsel / Getty Images 55tr, Jamie McDonald / Getty Images 55crb, Stefan Pielow 19tr; Kit Houghton / Houghton's Horses: Kit Houghton 48–49; Bob Langrish: Bob Langrish 4clb, 4bl, 5tr, 10bl, 24l, 47bc, 52–53, 53cr, 53crb, 57br, 59tl. All other images © Dorling Kindersley. For further information see: www.dkimages.com